E1

M

Princess
Elizabeth

E1

Princess
Margaret

PLATE 1

E2

E2

E2

Tom Tierney

Princess Elizabeth

E2

PLATE 2

E3

Tom Tierney

Princess
Elizabeth

E3

Tom Tierney

Lieutenant
Philip Mountbatten

P1

PLATE 3

E3

fold train
forward

fold train
forward

PLATE 4

E3

E3

PLATE 5

Princess
Anne

The Queen Mother

Prince
Charles

PLATE 6

P1

E3

E3

P1

fold train
forward

PLATE 7

PLATE 8

PLATE 9

Ed

E4

A

Prince
Edward

Queen Elizabeth

E4

Prince Philip

P2

Prince
Andrew

PLATE 10

E4

E4

E4

PLATE 11

PLATE 12

Prince
Philip

P3

Queen Elizabeth

E5

Charles, Prince of Wales

Prince
William

Prince
Henry

PLATE 13

Princess
Anne

Andrew,
Duke of York

Prince
Edward

Zara Phillips    Peter Phillips    Eugenie    Beatrice

PLATE 14

D

S

Diana,
Princess of Wales

Sarah,
Duchess of York

PLATE 15

E5

E5

E5

PLATE 16